Presented to:

_____

From:

_____

On this date:

_____

This book is dedicated to our parents,
Roy and Linda Drake and Art and Anne Land,
for showing us the way to the Savior.

Published by B&H Publishing Group, Nashville, Tennessee

Illustrations by Diana Lawrence, Copyright © 2020 by B&H Publishing Group

Scripture quotations are taken from the Christian Standard Bible®,
Copyright © 2017 by Holman Bible Publishers.
Used by permission. Christian Standard Bible® and CSB® are
federally registered trademarks of Holman Bible Publishers.

DEWEY: 242.34 SUBHD: DEVOTIONAL LITERATURE / EASTER / LENT

Printed in Shenzhen, Guangdong, China, October 2019

1 2 3 4 5 6 • 23 22 21 20 19

The Way to the Savior

A FAMILY EASTER DEVOTIONAL

Jeff and Abbey Land

B&H kids

Nashville TN

Dear Parents,

As you begin this book, it's important to know how to talk to your children about Lent. Lent is the forty-day season between Ash Wednesday and Easter. It is a time set apart by liturgical churches to pray, fast, and remember what Jesus did for believers at Calvary. Lent doesn't have to be specific to any denomination, so in recent years, more and more evangelical churches have begun participating in Lent.

Your family can use the Lenten season to thoughtfully remember Jesus' life, death, and resurrection. The chapters in this book will focus you on several aspects of what it means to follow Christ— hope, love, thanksgiving, commitment, forgiveness, trust, and obedience. As each Easter season approaches, begin sharing *The Way to the Savior* as a family. Read the devotions, discuss the Cross Connections, read Scripture, pray together, and remember Jesus' last days and resurrection. This time spent together as a family can be somewhat sacrificial since time will be taken away from other daily activities to focus on Jesus and His sacrifice.

Explain to your children that many people give up something during Lent as a reminder of Christ giving His life for us. Kids might choose to give up candy or sweets or a favorite video game. Or you might encourage your kids to add something instead. They could choose to spend the forty days being kinder to each other, focusing on obeying rules, or even choosing to do their homework without complaining. You might choose to give up things as a family as well. You can make this journey your own and create a unique season that is personal, meaningful, and faith-building for those you love.

Neither kids nor adults are always perfect at making sacrifices for Lent. If family members mess up, let it be a reminder that Jesus gave His life on the cross as an act of mercy for the lost. He loved people so much that He died to give them forgiveness of sins.

Let us enter this season with thoughtfulness and praise as we share the way to the Savior!

Love in Christ,

Jeff and Abbey Land

"For I know the plans I have for you. . . . plans for your well-being, not for disaster, to give you a future and a HOPE."

—Jeremiah 29:11

Hope

The prophets promised that hope would come in the form of the Savior, Jesus Christ.

Hope No Matter What

Job was a successful man with a wonderful family, home, and life. He loved God, and God blessed him. Then everything fell apart as God allowed Satan to test Job. Job lost his children, his animals, and his servants. God allowed Satan to go one step further and put painful sores all over Job's body. Incredibly miserable, Job found himself questioning why he was even born.

Job's friend Zophar visited him and offered the words you see in Job 11:18. He encouraged Job not to give up.

No matter what Job was going through, he could have hope in God. You can have that same hope and know that God is in control of your life. He sent Jesus to earth to die on the cross for you, and He is always watching over you.

Sometimes you might want to give up, but think about Job. He lost everything yet still believed God would be faithful. Even when life is difficult and everything seems to go wrong, you can always have hope in God.

Dear God,
I want to have the same hope Job did. Help me to understand that no matter what, I can have hope in You. Amen.

CROSS CONNECTION

Have you ever hoped for something you didn't believe would happen? How do you think that hope is different from the hope Job had? How did Jesus dying on the cross for your sins affect the hope you have?

You will be confident,
because there is HOPE.
You will look carefully about
and lie down in safety.—JOB 11:18

But look, the LORD keeps his eye on those who fear him—those who depend on his faithful love. —PSALM 33:18

Depend on God

Someday, when you start driving, a parent will probably say to you, "Keep your eyes on the road." Why? Because it's important to stay alert and know what's ahead. Maybe you have heard a baseball coach say, "Keep your eye on the ball." If you don't keep your eye on the ball, you won't be able to hit it. The Bible reminds you that God has His eyes on *you*. Why would God choose to keep His eyes on you? Because you are important to Him!

You can depend on God, whatever you are going through. When you hope in Him, you are aware of His attention and protection. Even when you aren't thinking about God, He is there. That's a promise God has made that won't be broken.

God also promised to send a Savior to earth to give hope to everyone who believes in Him. Do you know someone who needs to know about this hope? As Easter Sunday approaches, think about someone you know who needs to hear more about the hope Jesus offers to all people.

Dear God,
Thank You for Your promises and for having Your eyes always on me. Help me to put my hope in You no matter what. Amen.

CROSS CONNECTION

Make a list of people you know who might need to hear about the hope of Jesus. Pray about your list, and make plans to invite someone to Easter services with you.

Waiting for God

Waiting can be hard, and you have to wait a lot in life! You have to wait for recess, wait for food, wait for your birthday, and wait for vacation. When the apostle Paul wrote a letter to the church in Galatia, his advice was to wait. Why would Paul tell people to wait?

Paul shared that waiting and having faith would give people the hope they needed. People waited a long time for the promised Savior to come to earth. Jesus came to offer hope to all those who had waited for His arrival. This same promise is made to you as well. Wait and have faith, and God will provide the hope you need to live a life that is pleasing to God. Waiting may be hard, but the rewards Paul promised are far better than any waiting you have to do.

The next time you are waiting in a long line at an amusement park or carnival, think about how Paul told people they had to wait. And as fun as the ride may be, it is nothing compared to waiting for God and His glory.

Dear God,
Help me remember that waiting is okay. Thank You for providing people in my life who help me while I eagerly wait for the things You promised in the Bible. Amen.

CROSS CONNECTION

As a family, rate each member on a scale of 1 to 10 on how good he or she is at waiting. Talk about how you can be a better wait-er. But *don't* wait to invite others to join you in celebrating Jesus' resurrection on Easter!

For we eagerly await through the Spirit, by faith, the HOPE of righteousness.
—GALATIANS 5:5

*I have a HOPE in God,
which these men themselves
also accept, that there will
be a resurrection, both of
the righteous and the
unrighteous.*
—ACTS 24:15

Stand Strong with Hope

The card on the package read, "I hope you have a happy Easter! Love, Mom." The person who wrote the card wanted her daughter to enjoy the celebration of Jesus' resurrection from death. This mother was hopeful that her much-loved daughter would have a happy, special day.

In the book of Acts, Paul wrote about hope too. He wanted to give a simple but important message to the people in the church: he had hope in God. Paul was sharing his hope with others because he wanted them to stand strong and experience the same hope he had. Paul knew he could have hope in God because God is all-powerful, all-knowing, and perfect. God can be trusted. What about you? Do you have the kind of hope in God that Paul had?

Dear God,
Help me have hope in You. I want to share this hope with others. Show me how to share hope as Paul did. Amen.

CROSS CONNECTION

Send a letter to someone and wish him or her a happy Easter season. Include a note about the hope found in Jesus!

15

Put Your Hope in Grace

What's the last thing you hoped for? Was it a good grade, good weather, or your favorite food to be cooked for dinner? Maybe you hoped your favorite team would win the championship. Did you get what you hoped for? Sometimes in life you hope for something but what you get isn't exactly what you had hoped for. With God, things are different. When you place your hope in Him, you can know that He will deliver. He is the source of hope.

The most important person in whom you can ever have hope is Jesus Christ. That hope is brought to you through the grace Jesus offers because He suffered and died on the cross for you and your sins. The hope you have is because of the free gift given by Jesus. If you ask, you will receive from Jesus; it's that simple! That's what grace is: something you can't earn; it's given freely.

Dear God,
Thank You for grace. I know I don't deserve what Jesus did for me. Help me remember to put my hope in Jesus. Amen.

CROSS CONNECTION

What hope do you have in Jesus? What do you know about Jesus that makes you want to trust Him with your struggles and with your future?

Therefore, with your minds ready for action, be sober-minded and set your HOPE completely on the grace to be brought to you at the revelation of Jesus Christ.—1 PETER 1:13

Love

For God LOVED the world in this way:
He gave his one and only Son,
so that everyone who believes in him
will not perish but have eternal life.

—JOHN 3:16

God loves people so much that He sent His Son, Jesus, to earth to be crucified for our sins.

If I speak human or angelic tongues but do not have LOVE, I am a noisy gong or a clanging cymbal. —1 CORINTHIANS **13:1**

Not Just Talk

Imagine a musician repeatedly crashing two cymbals together. If you heard that over and over, how would it sound? Probably just loud and empty. That's what Paul said a life without love would be like. Jesus is the perfect example of love. He spent His whole ministry teaching about how God loves people and wants them to have a relationship with Him.

When the time came for Jesus to be crucified, He could have used His power as the Son of God to avoid enduring such cruelty and pain, but He didn't. Jesus physically showed His love by dying on the cross for the sins of all who would believe in Him. He was not just talking when He said He loved people. He showed it.

What about you? Are you just "clanging cymbals" together, or do your actions show your love for others? You don't have to die on a cross, but your actions can make a difference in sharing God's love with others.

Dear God,
Thank You for showing Your love for me. Help my love for others to be evident and heartfelt too. Amen.

CROSS CONNECTION

Why do you think showing love to others is important?
Who in your life needs to be shown God's love today?

"Do You Still Love Me?"

With big tears in his eyes and streaming down his cheeks, my son looked at me and said, "Do you still love me?" He had just spilled an entire box of cereal on the floor and made a big mess. He thought I wouldn't love him anymore. I grabbed a broom and said, "Of course I love you! No matter what you spill on the kitchen floor! Now, let's work together to get this cleaned up."

This story may sound silly, but sometimes people are the same way about God and think His love depends on how good we are—or aren't! But the Bible promises that God's love is unconditional. Day after day, year after year, He continues to wondrously show his faithful love to us . . . no matter what. He sent His Son as a gift, even though He knew we would continue to sin and need His mercy. He knew He would continue to love us, no matter what.

Dear God,
Please forgive me of my sins. Thank You for continuing to show Your faithful love to me. Amen.

CROSS CONNECTION

Ask each family member, "Do you love me?" Pay attention to how it feels when you hear "Yes" as the answer. Now, how does it feel to know that God loves you even more?

I have loved you with an everlasting LOVE; *therefore,
I have continued to extend faithful* LOVE *to you.*

—JEREMIAH **31:3**

But God proves his own LOVE
for us in that while we were
still sinners, Christ died for us.

—ROMANS 5:8

Prove It

Which came first, the chicken or the egg? How do you know for sure? If you think you know the answer, are you able to prove it? When you write down an answer to a math problem, are you required to *prove* how you got the answer by showing your work? When you show your work, you are proving to the teacher that you understand the concept being taught to you.

Today's Scripture is a reminder that God proved His love by sending His one and only Son, Jesus, to die for our sins. Because God is the Creator of everything, He doesn't have to prove anything to anybody, but He did. You never have to doubt whether you are loved. The sacrifice God made is proof of His love for you. God knew you would mess up and sin, and He still chose to offer you the gift of eternal life.

Dear God,
Thank You for proving Your love and for loving me even when my actions are unlovable. Amen.

CROSS CONNECTION

Talk about ways you can prove to others that you love Jesus. How can the things you do each day show Jesus to others?

Your All

Do you have a favorite game, a show you can't go a week without watching, or a sport you always think about? When we love to learn about something and spend time on it, we often give it our *all*.

What does the word *all* mean to you? It can mean *everything*, *anything*, or *giving your best*. The Bible says you are supposed to love God with your *all*. That means you should love God more than you love anything or anyone else.

Sometimes it might be hard to think about loving God more than you love your mom or dad, but the Bible says God is above everything. He wants you to love Him more than you love your hobbies, your pets, your friends and family, and even yourself. Loving God with all your heart, soul, mind, and strength means you want and try to put God first in your life. At Easter and all throughout the year, He deserves your all!

Dear God,
Help me to know when I am loving something more than I am loving You.
You should be first in my life. Amen.

CROSS CONNECTION

Name five things you love. How much time do you spend focusing on those things? Read Mark 12:30 again and ask God to help you live out this verse.

LOVE *the Lord your God with all your heart,*
with all your soul, with all your mind,
and with all your strength.—MARK 12:30

No one has greater LOVE than this: to lay down his life for his friends.

—John 15:13

Lay Down Your Life

Read today's verse several times. Wow! Those are pretty powerful words. It says that laying down your life for your friends is the greatest way to show love. That sounds pretty intense.

Throughout history there have been stories of people who have given their own lives to save others. You might have heard a story about a parent who gave her life to save her children during a natural disaster. This is love. This is intense love.

Jesus loves you with this kind of intense love. He gave up His life because He loves you so much. The love of Jesus is far superior to any you've ever experienced on earth. If you don't know Jesus as your Savior and Lord of your life, ask your parent or church leader any questions you have about Jesus and a relationship with Him. You don't ever have to wonder whether Jesus loves you; He loves you more than you'll ever understand.

Dear God,
Thank You for loving me. Thank You for Jesus, who gave His life for me. Help me lay down my life for You each day. Amen.

CROSS CONNECTION

Can you name someone you know who is gifted at showing intense love for others? What's *your* favorite way to show love?

Thanksgiving

Enter his gates with THANKSGIVING *and his courts with praise. Give* THANKS *to him and bless his name.* —Psalm 100:4

Even up to the Last Supper, Jesus lived an example of giving thanks.

Give Thanks

When you picture a table filled with ham, deviled eggs, and coconut cake, what special holiday comes to mind? These foods are often eaten at Easter dinner, a time when families come together to celebrate the holiday. Some families use this special day to gather for reunions or an annual egg hunt.

But Easter is more than a day to eat delicious food with loved ones and to eat candy; it's a time to give thanks for the sacrifice Jesus made on the cross. Being thankful is biblical. This means the Bible says to be thankful all the time, not just on certain days. You have many reasons to be thankful, and the most important reason is Jesus. Jesus' death on the cross provides you with the opportunity to choose to spend eternity with Him. That's definitely something you can be thankful for!

Dear God,
Thank You for all the blessings in my life, especially Jesus! You are amazing, and I'm thankful for everything You've done for me. Amen.

CROSS CONNECTION

Make a list of things in God's creation for which you are most thankful.

"Give **THANKS** to the L*ORD*; proclaim his name! Make his works known among the peoples. Declare that his name is exalted." —I*SAIAH* **12:4**

I offer **THANKS** *and praise
to you, God of my fathers,
because you have given
me wisdom and power.*

—DANIEL 2:23

Prayers of Thankfulness

In the book of Daniel in the Bible, Daniel was obedient to God's directions, so God gave Daniel wisdom and power to interpret the dreams of King Nebuchadnezzar. When Daniel recognized what God had done for him, he was thankful and praised God. Daniel is a great example of how we can respond to answered prayer. We can be thankful and praise God for what He's done.

Sometimes our prayers are answered the way we hoped, like Daniel's prayers.

Other times, God's answer to our prayers is much different than we expected. Either way, it is important to be grateful that God is always listening.

Spending time in prayer, and filling those prayers with thankfulness, is a great way to connect more closely with God. He may not answer our prayers the way we hope, but we can always be grateful to Him for His love and for sending our Savior to earth!

Dear God,
Thank You for hearing my prayers. Help me to remember that You always hear me and want me to talk to You. Amen.

CROSS CONNECTION

Take some time as a family to thank God for the things He has done for you. Challenge yourselves to spend the days of Lent with hearts full of thankfulness.

A Thank-You Letter

When you receive a nice gift, the polite thing to do is write a letter of thanks. You might mention a reason you like the gift, how much you appreciate the gift, and ways you will use it. Sometimes you might have found it hard to write a thank-you letter because you didn't need the gift or you already owned one like it. Your parents probably told you to be thankful that you got anything at all.

God's gift to you is different. . . . You definitely needed it, and you didn't already own it. He gave you the greatest gift you'll ever receive—His Son, Jesus. Jesus gave you an amazing gift as well—His life for your sins. Jesus chose to die on the cross for you. He didn't stay dead, though. He came back to life three days later. Jesus suffered and died to give you the opportunity to have eternal life. How have you shown your gratefulness for these indescribable gifts?

Dear God,
Thank You for Jesus, the greatest gift ever. Thank You for loving me no matter what. Thank You for the gift of eternal life. Amen.

CROSS CONNECTION

As a family, write a thank-You letter to Jesus. Thank Him for His great gift—His sacrifice on the cross. Tell Him how you plan to use this gift for Him.

THANKS *be to God for his indescribable gift!*

—2 CORINTHIANS 9:15

I give **THANKS** *to my God for every remembrance of you.* —Philippians 1:3

Paul's Thankfulness

For whom are you thankful? Why are you grateful for that person? Have you told the person you are thankful for him or her and why? Telling friends or family members that you appreciate them makes them feel valued. It helps them know you care.

Paul wanted to let the people of Philippi know he was thankful for them, so he wrote them a letter in the book of Philippians. How do you think the people felt when they read Paul's words?

Paul wanted those who believed in Jesus to know he was thankful they were part of his life and his mission.

Spending time with people who also love Jesus can be encouraging to you. Worshiping together with other believers on Easter is a time to be thankful for Jesus' sacrifice and for your friendships with others who believe in Jesus too. Remember and be thankful for those who love God like you do.

Dear God,
I'm thankful for the people You've put in my life to encourage me and to help me serve You. Help me show my thanks to others. Amen.

CROSS CONNECTION

Who are the people you are thankful for? How can you tell them this week?

Words of Thanks

At the Last Supper, Jesus knew what was about to happen. He would soon be betrayed by one of His disciples and sacrificed on the cross. But instead of Jesus' words being full of anger or fear, He led the disciples in giving thanks for the bread and the cup. He chose words of gratefulness.

Words matter! When your words are angry, ungrateful, or discouraging, they can hurt others. But did you know those words also hurt you? When you allow your mind and speech to be filled with anger and bitterness, it's a reflection of your heart. Instead of saying hurtful or discouraging things, God wants you to speak words of kindness and graciousness, as Jesus did.

On the days leading up to Easter (and the days after too!), make it your goal to fill your mind and your speech with words of thanks.

Dear God,
Help me to choose my words wisely. I want the words I say to show others how thankful I am for You and Your Son, Jesus. Amen.

CROSS CONNECTION
Gather the family, and take turns sharing reasons you are thankful for each other.

And he took bread, gave THANKS,
*broke it, gave it to them, and said,
"This is my body, which is given for
you. Do this in remembrance of me."*
—LUKE 22:19

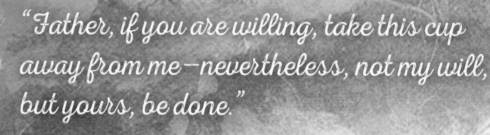

"*Father, if you are willing, take this cup away from me—nevertheless, not my will, but yours, be done.*"

—LUKE 22:42

Commitment

Jesus' coming crucifixion weighed heavily on His earthly mind. His divine being, however, was committed to dying on the cross for our sins.

Committing Your List

How many activities do you do in one day? How about one week? A month? An entire year? Your list is probably incredibly long. God wants you to give everything you do to Him. Whatever you plan to do, choose to dedicate it to God first.

Think about what it will look like to commit your activities to the Lord. If you play baseball, you might commit to being a godly encourager to your teammates.

If you love to read, you might commit to reading your Bible first, before spending time in your favorite library book.

When you choose to give everything to God, He is in control of your life. God wants only what is best for you. That's why He sent His Son, Jesus, to earth. God wanted you to have the choice to commit your life to Him forever. When you are faithful to God in your life, God will honor your actions.

Dear God,
I want You to be in control of my life. Take control of all my activities so I may honor You. Amen.

CROSS CONNECTION

Make a list of your activities. Can you think of ways to commit each of them to God?

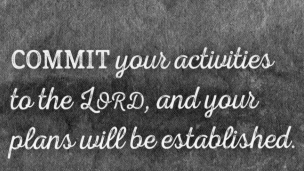

COMMIT *your activities to the LORD, and your plans will be established.*

—PROVERBS 16:3

He did not COMMIT sin, and no deceit was found in his mouth. —1 Peter 2:22

No Sin Found

Sin is anything you do that doesn't please God. Every single person who walks on earth has sinned, except one. Jesus lived on this earth, yet He never sinned. He never said anything wrong or did anything to displease God!

Will you commit to being more like Jesus and trying not to sin? No matter how hard you try, you will still make mistakes. You will still say things that aren't pleasing to God, but God will still love you. God wants you to do your best and remember Jesus is the best example to follow in how to live your life.

The devil will sometimes make sin look enticing. Remember, he tricked Adam and Eve into thinking they needed the forbidden fruit. You will give in to temptation from time to time, but if you ask, God will forgive you.

Dear God,
Thank You for sending Jesus as the perfect example for me to follow. Help my actions and words be pleasing to You. Amen.

CROSS CONNECTION

What sins do you struggle with? How do you try to avoid temptation?

Definitely Devoted

In the spring, flowers bloom everywhere. Did you know that many of those flowers come from bulbs that were planted in the fall? Long before spring arrives, the bulbs are planted and mulched and watered. When they begin to grow, the flowers need to be weeded, watered, and even fertilized with special plant food to help them grow. Gardeners must be devoted, or committed, to caring for the plants for them to grow strong and beautiful.

God wants you to be devoted to Him. How? By studying the Bible, going to church to learn more about Him, spending time with other believers, keeping God's commandments, and praying. The goal is to be devoted to God no matter what happens in your life. When Jesus came to earth, He was devoted to spreading the news about God. Devote your life to God too—commit to grow closer to Him!

Dear God,
I want to be devoted to You in what I say and do. Help me make good decisions that honor You. Amen.

CROSS CONNECTION

Why do you think God wants you to be devoted, or committed, to serving and loving Him?

*Be wholeheartedly devoted to the L*ORD *our God to walk in his statutes and to keep his commands, as it is today.* —1 KINGS 8:61

Take delight in the LORD, and he
will give you your heart's desires.
—PSALM 37:4

Your Heart's Desires

What if you were given permission to eat as much Easter candy as you wanted? And what if you wanted a lot? How do you think you'd feel later? You probably would have a stomachache, even though you'd received exactly what you wanted.

Often the things we desire (popularity and comfort and all the things other kids have) are not always what are best for us. God's plans are so much better. When we follow God's plan for our lives, the rewards are far greater than anything we could want on our own. God wants to give us what our hearts desire, but He loves when those desires grow our faith and make us closer to Him.

Choose to "take delight" in what God has planned for your life, and watch God's desires become your wants too. Commit your life to God and watch Him work in your life today. You will never get too much of God!

Dear God,
Thank You for wanting the best for my life. Show me how to desire a life that's committed to You. Amen.

CROSS CONNECTION

What is one way you can choose to show God you are committed to serving Him?

51

Always Seek God

Do you know what *seek* means? You've probably played hide-and-seek. When you "seek," you are looking for someone. You are trying to find someone. Do you seek God? Seeking God means you are looking for Him.

In Psalm 31:1, David, the writer of most of the book of Psalms, was crying out to God. He knew God could save him in times of trouble. David was seeking God because he was committed to living a life that pleased and honored Him.

Whom do you seek when you need help? Follow David's example. Commit your life to following God. Look for Him every day. God's plan for your life included sacrificing His only Son to save you from suffering for your sins eternally. You can be like David and take refuge in God. Seek God when you need help, and you can know God will answer you.

Dear God,
Thank You for being my safe place to turn when I need You. Thank You for always listening to me when I call to You. Amen.

CROSS CONNECTION

Do you have a time set aside each day when you seek God? How can your family join together to seek God every day?

LORD, I seek refuge in you;
let me never be disgraced.
Save me by your righteousness.

—Psalm 31:1

Forgiveness

Jesus said, "Father, FORGIVE them, because they do not know what they are doing." —Luke 23:34

The way to true forgiveness is made available only through the blood of Jesus.

If you FORGIVE *others their offenses,
your heavenly Father will forgive you
as well. But if you don't forgive others,
your Father will not forgive your offenses.*

—MATTHEW 6:14–15

Give It to Get It

A master had a servant who owed him a huge sum of money. The master demanded the servant repay him. When the servant begged for mercy, the master forgave all the man owed him.

The same servant then went to another man who owed him just a small amount of money. The other man begged for mercy, but the servant would not forgive the money he was owed. The master heard about this, and he was so angry that he had the servant thrown in jail.

God promised forgiveness of sins when He sent Jesus to the earth. Even though you didn't do anything to deserve God's forgiveness, He freely offers it to you. Today's verse is a reminder that because the gift of forgiveness is free, we should also be quick to forgive those who have wronged us.

Dear God,
Thank You for the gift of Jesus Christ. Your forgiveness is better than I could ever ask from You. Help me to forgive other people as You have forgiven me.
Amen.

CROSS CONNECTION
Whom do you need to forgive this Easter season?

Ultimate Forgiveness

I once had a teacher at church who would pray for the afflicted every Sunday morning. I wasn't sure what it meant, but I felt like having an "affliction" must be really bad.

I later learned that an *affliction* is when someone is hurt or ill from a disease or accident. People who are afflicted are suffering and need relief. The psalmist in Psalm 25:18 was begging God to ease his afflictions and trouble and to forgive his sins as well.

When you have days that feel full of affliction or a heart that seems full of regret, remember you can always call on Jesus for help and mercy. He suffered affliction during His days on earth, and He too reached to God for encouragement. God is the ultimate encourager and will offer you forgiveness when you ask Him.

Dear God,
Sometimes I just feel overwhelmed. Please help me remember that You have paid the price for all my sins with Your Son, Jesus. Thank You for loving me. Amen.

CROSS CONNECTION
Why is it important to ask God for forgiveness?

Consider my affliction and trouble,
and FORGIVE all my sins.
—Psalm 25:18

LORD, if you kept an account of iniquities, Lord,
who could stand? But with you there is FORGIVENESS,
so that you may be revered. I wait for the LORD;
I wait and put my hope in his word. —Psalm 130:3–5

Don't Count on It

One, two, three . . . Think of all the times you've messed up this week. Did you forget to clean your room? Did you yell at your brother or sister when they touched your video game? Did you talk back to your mom or dad? Try to add up the number of times you've done things you know were wrong this week.

Everyone messes up. Every. Single. Day. That's called sin. Everyone sins. God knew people would need a Savior, and He sent Jesus, His Son, to come to earth so that people would have the opportunity to be forgiven of their sins.

Today's Scripture is a reminder that people mess up all the time, but God in His mercy doesn't keep track of how many times we mess up. If you believe in God and ask Him to forgive you, the Bible says He will. You can have forgiveness because Jesus paid the sacrifice for your sins.

Dear God,
Thank You for not counting all the times I've sinned. Help me to remember that You are a forgiving God. Thank You for Jesus and His sacrifice. Amen.

CROSS CONNECTION
How does it make you feel to know God forgives and forgets your sins once you've asked for forgiveness?

I'll Get You Back

When another person hurts you, it's frustrating. Maybe a friend deliberately says something mean about you, or maybe someone physically hurts you. You might think, *I'll get you back*.

The Bible says that before we pray, we should think about the people we have a grudge against. A *grudge* is holding on to anger toward someone for doing something harmful to us in the past. Holding grudges isn't healthy. Instead of holding a grudge, we should forgive that person. When we do, it means that God will also forgive us when we ask Him.

Jesus is a great example of forgiveness. He forgives people for their sins—when they ask—even though they don't deserve it. He wants people to come to Him with pure hearts and honest intentions. Is there someone you need to forgive today?

Dear God,
You are a forgiving God. You forgive me even though I don't deserve it. Help me to forgive people I need to forgive. I want to follow Jesus' example. Amen.

CROSS CONNECTION
Are you holding a grudge against anyone? What is a healthy way to deal with those feelings?

Whenever you stand praying, if you have anything against anyone, **FORGIVE** him, so that your Father in heaven will also forgive you your wrongdoing.

—MARK **11:25**

Peter replied, "Repent and be baptized, each of you, in the name of Jesus Christ for the FORGIVENESS of your sins, and you will receive the gift of the Holy Spirit." —ACTS 2:38

Receiving Forgiveness

Jesus wants you to experience His forgiveness. The Bible says that God will forgive you of your sins if you admit you are a sinner. Admitting you are a sinner means you know you do things against God and you want to make changes in your life to please God.

Next, you need to believe that Jesus is God's Son. When you do, you are saying, "I believe that Jesus is the Savior. He is the one true God."

Finally, you have to confess that Jesus is your Savior. You are saying that you don't want to be in control of your life. You want to let Jesus be the boss of your life instead.

Do you want to receive Jesus as your Lord and Savior? Jesus dying on the cross and being raised from the dead is the whole purpose of Easter.

Dear God,
Thank You for Jesus. Thank You that He is the Savior. Help me remember that Jesus will forgive my sins. Amen.

CROSS CONNECTION

Take some time tonight to talk to your children about what it means to be a Christian. If appropriate for their age, lead them in the steps of becoming a Christian and pray with them.

Trust

The LORD is my strength and my shield;
my heart TRUSTS in him, and I am helped.
Therefore my heart celebrates, and I give
thanks to him with my song. —PSALM 28:7

*Our resurrected and powerful
Lord is victorious over death,
and He is worthy of our trust.*

TRUST *in the* L O R D *with all your heart,*
and do not rely on your own understanding;
in all your ways know him,
and he will make your paths straight.

—P ROVERBS 3:5–6

Give God Your All

When you are getting ready for a big event or competition, you might hear your parents say, "Give it your all!" or "Give 100 percent!" That means they want you to try your hardest to win.

Today's scripture is a reminder that when you choose to put your trust in God, you should trust Him with your whole life and give Him your all. That might be hard. You might ask God to help you earn a certain position on your team or a role in the play. Or you may pray that your dad gets that promotion at work. But no matter God's answer, you have to trust He knows what He is doing. God has a plan.

Even Jesus trusted that God knew the perfect plan for His life. When Jesus was sacrificed on the cross, He placed His trust in God and gave His all. Jesus is the perfect example for you to follow. You can trust God too.

Dear God,
Thank You for being trustworthy. Help me not to worry about what is happening in my life but to trust You to have a plan. Amen.

CROSS CONNECTION

When was the last time you really had to trust someone? Why might you have trouble trusting in God?

Your Rescuer

The headline read, "Man Saves Child, Woman from Near-Drowning in the Arkansas River." Wow! A man risked his own life twice to pull two people out of the river. Neither the child nor the woman realized how swiftly the river was flowing. They both slipped and fell into the water. The man reacted quickly both times, helping each person to safety.

Would you have jumped into a river to save a stranger? Jesus performed an even bigger rescue. He didn't just risk His life for you; Jesus gave it. Fully. Jesus knew you would sin, and if He didn't come to earth, you would suffer from the consequences of your sins forever. Because He wanted people to be forgiven of their sins, He willingly hung on the cross and endured physical pain. The people yelled at Him and mocked Him. But Jesus knew He was on the cross for a good reason. *You* are the reason. Jesus wants you to know God and trust Him to rescue you.

Dear God,
Thank You for Jesus. He took the punishment for my sin. Help me to trust Jesus
fully as my Lord and Savior. Amen.

CROSS CONNECTION

Why is it impossible for you to save yourself from death? How does it make you feel to know you can trust Jesus to rescue those who believe in Him?

He **TRUSTS** in God;
let God rescue him now—
if he takes pleasure in him!
For he said, "I am the Son
of God."—MATTHEW 27:43

Then the one seated on the throne said, "Look, I am making everything new." He also said, "Write, because these words are faithful and true." —REVELATION 21:5

He Makes All Things New

Have you ever totally bombed something, like a school assignment or a tryout for a play or team? Maybe you made a terrible grade on a test or missed the winning goal for the soccer championship. The pressure can be terrible. You didn't want to let anyone down, but you felt like everything was your fault. If only you had studied harder, practiced longer, or tried harder. You really wanted a do-over.

Jesus came to earth, shared His message, died on the cross, and rose again. Then He ascended to heaven. The Bible promises that when Jesus comes again, He will make all things new. Not only will there be no more disappointments, but this world of disease, crime, and poverty will go away. You can trust that God will make all things new and perfect again. No one knows when, but God always keeps His promises.

Dear God,
You promised that You will make all things new one day. Help me to trust in Your promises. Thank You for loving me! Amen.

CROSS CONNECTION

What is one thing you wish you could do over or make new? Why is it important to trust that God will fulfill the promises in the Bible?

Always Trust God

But what if everyone laughs at me? Have you ever had that thought? Maybe you were about to go onstage as part of the Easter musical at church, and you were nervous. You might trip or forget your lines or get sick. All those situations could be scary!

When Jesus was faced with dying on the cross, do you think He was afraid? He had never physically died before, and now He knew that was the plan.

Jesus willingly offered Himself as a sacrifice for you as part of God's plan. He chose to die because He trusted God's plan. You can trust God's plan for your life too. You don't ever have to wonder whether you can trust God. He is always there for you when you call on Him. When you are afraid, you can turn to God for help. God does not promise that you'll never be afraid; He does promise you will always be able to trust in Him.

Dear God,
Help me remember I can always turn to You for help. And help me remember to trust You with everything in my life. Amen.

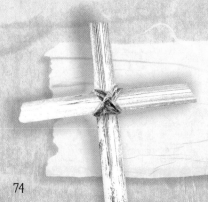

CROSS CONNECTION

Talk about God's plan for Jesus' death and resurrection. Did the plan work? Why might we sometimes have trouble trusting God with His plan for our own lives?

When I am afraid, I will **TRUST** *in you.*

—Psalm 56:3

The fear of mankind is a snare, but the one who TRUSTS *in the* LORD *is protected.*

—PROVERBS 29:25

Protective Gear

Easter is always in the spring. During spring, flowers start to bloom, but sometimes they bloom when the nights are still quite chilly outside. You might have seen people putting blankets or sheets over their plants and wondered why they were doing that. When a dangerous frost is predicted, the sheets are used to keep the plants safe from the frost. If the sheets didn't protect the plants, they would die from the cold temperatures.

The Bible promises that the one who trusts in the Lord is protected and able to withstand the dangers of mankind. Many things in the world might be tempting to you, but God promises to protect you. You can know that God will keep you safe, even when you don't get everything right. Don't be afraid to put your trust in Jesus. Remember, He was victorious over death. He is fully able to protect you and worthy of your trust.

Dear God,
Thank You for being trustworthy. I'm grateful that no matter what I face, I can trust that You will protect me. You are my true protection. Amen.

CROSS CONNECTION

What have you been afraid of in the past? Name some times when you've chosen to trust in God's protection.

"Go, therefore, and make disciples of all nations, baptizing them in the name of the Father and of the Son and of the Holy Spirit, teaching them to observe everything I have commanded you."

—MATTHEW 28:19–20

Obedience

After Jesus was resurrected, He gave the disciples a command to continue Christ's message of salvation. People obey that same command today.

For the time has come for judgment to begin with God's household, and if it begins with us, what will the outcome be for those who **DISOBEY** the gospel of God?—1 Peter 4:17

Consequences

Mom reminded her son, "Today's decisions affect tomorrow's choices." What did she mean? She meant that the decisions her son makes today will limit or change the choices he has later. Think about it like this: your mom and dad tell you that you can go to a friend's house tomorrow if you clean your room today. If you don't clean your room, your parents won't let you go to your friend's house tomorrow. That's called a consequence of disobedience.

In today's Scripture, Peter was reminding people that there would be consequences for disobeying the gospel of God. The Bible says those who believe the gospel and make Jesus their Savior will be saved and will live eternally in heaven. When a person chooses to disobey the gospel, the consequence of that decision lasts forever. Although Jesus' death could save everyone who ever lived, only those who choose to believe Him and obey will spend forever in heaven.

Dear God,
Help me to obey Your gospel. Thank You for providing a way for me to spend eternity with You. Amen.

CROSS CONNECTION

What are some consequences you've experienced lately? What is a good consequence of believing in Jesus as your Savior?

Running with the Wrong Crowd

Sometimes obeying your parents is hard, and you might think they are being too strict when they say, "Don't hang out there" or "Watch who you spend time with." However, your parents want the best for your life, a life that is spent following Christ. They know that even though you might want to do good, when you run with the wrong crowd, you might be persuaded to make bad decisions.

In Galatians 5:7, Paul was writing to the church at Galatia and was basically saying what your parents tell you. He was asking the people, "Who are you spending time with?" He knew someone had been a bad influence on the people of Galatia and had told them lies about God . . . lies the Galatians had believed. Paul wanted the people to remember that they should follow the truth of God instead of the wrong crowd. Whose truth are you following?

Dear God,
Help me to follow Your truth. Help me make good decisions and choose friends that point me to You. Amen.

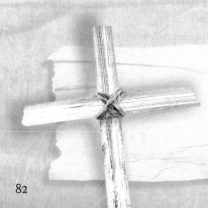

CROSS CONNECTION

Think about the people you choose to be around. Are those people helping you make good decisions? How do your friends affect what you choose to say and do?

You were running well.
Who prevented you from being
persuaded regarding the TRUTH?
—GALATIANS 5:7

Who among you fears the LORD and listens to his servant? Who among you walks in darkness, and has no light? Let him trust in the name of the LORD; let him lean on his God. —ISAIAH 50:10

Turn Up the Light

When Jesus died on the cross, the land went completely dark in the middle of the day. Imagine being in a completely dark room. Your eyes are open, but everything is black. You need to find the way out, but someone tells you that the room is full of traps! Uh-oh. You don't want to move an inch. Now, imagine that someone in the room lights a candle. The light is dim, but you can see well enough to safely navigate your way to the exit.

Walking through life without Jesus is like walking through a dark room with no way out. Not only is Jesus the light; He is the only way to eternal life. People who don't know Jesus may seem like they are happy; however, their happiness is only temporary. With Jesus, you will have joy for eternity. Things won't be perfect, but you will have the Lord—and His light—on your side.

Dear God,
Help me to always follow Your light in my life. Thank You for showing me the way. Amen.

CROSS CONNECTION

What are some things you are afraid of? How can you shine God's light on those fears this week and let Him walk you through them?

Even the Wind Obeys

Have you ever been scared during a storm? The wind blasts the trees back and forth. The lightning cracks wildly through the sky. The thunder roars so loudly that your whole house shakes. It can be terrifying.

Today's Bible reading comes from the story of Jesus and His disciples during a great storm at sea. The wind and the rain were beating up against their boat so strongly that the disciples feared the boat would sink and they would all drown. Jesus must have been scared too, right? Wrong! He was asleep! He was so asleep that the disciples had to wake Him up. He got up and simply said, "Silence! Be still!" Immediately the storm stopped.

Because Jesus was the authority, the storm listened to Him. The disciples were amazed that even the weather obeys Jesus. If the weather obeys Jesus, don't you think you should too?

Dear God,
You are so powerful! Help me to obey You each and every day. Amen.

CROSS CONNECTION

Think about the last time you called on God for help. Share what happened and how you felt. Spend time thanking God for always answering your cries.

Then he said to them, "Why are you afraid? Do you still have no faith?" And they were terrified and asked one another, "Who then is this? Even the wind and the sea OBEY him!" —Mark 4:40–41

The one who BELIEVES in the Son has eternal life, but the one who rejects the Son will not see life; instead, the wrath of God remains on him. —JOHN 3:36

One Way

The driver turned onto the road, and immediately other drivers started flashing their lights and honking their horns. The drivers seemed angry, but they were really worried because the driver had turned onto a one-way street and was going the wrong direction. He was seconds away from causing a dangerous car crash.

The Bible teaches that there is only one way to heaven—Jesus. If you choose not to obey what God says about salvation, not only will your life take a dangerous turn away from God, but you will also not experience the joy of heaven.

Without accepting Christ as your Savior, you will experience the punishment for sin. Do you know how to make Christ your Savior? If not, ask your parents what it means to obey Christ, and make Him the Lord of your life this Easter season.

Dear God,
Jesus is the Savior. Thank You for sending Him to take the punishment for my sin. I love You, God. Amen.

CROSS CONNECTION

What are some ways people think they might get to heaven? Why is it important to know there is only one way to get to heaven?

"See, the time is near. The Son of Man is betrayed into the hands of sinners."
—MATTHEW 26:45

Jesus' Last Days

As you come into this week before Easter, use these devotions to refocus your family on Christ's deep love for you.

READ MATTHEW 26:26–30

The Elements

Churches choose to observe the Lord's Supper in different ways and at different times throughout the year. At our church, the pastor calls the bread and grape juice we use the *elements* of the Lord's Supper. This practice began with Jesus, thousands of years ago, when He shared a final supper with His disciples.

Jesus knew it was almost time for Him to die on the cross, and He was preparing His disciples. First He showed them the bread and said it represented His body. Then He showed the disciples the cup that held the fruit of the vine and said it represented His blood. Imagine what the disciples might have been thinking as Jesus led them to eat and drink what was prepared for them. At this point, the disciples didn't fully understand what Jesus was about to go through. Something big was about to happen that would change the world forever.

Dear God,
Help me never forget what the bread and the cup represent—Jesus' blood and sacrifice on the cross for my sins. Amen.

CROSS CONNECTION

Review the Lord's Supper as a family. Talk about what each element means.

As they were eating, JESUS took bread, blessed and broke it, gave it to the disciples, and said, "Take and eat it; this is my body."
—MATTHEW 26:26

DAY
37

Going a little farther, he fell facedown and prayed, "My Father, if it is possible, let this cup pass from me. Yet not as I will, but as you will."

—Matthew 26:39

Are You Sure?

Have you ever known God wanted you to do something, but you prayed and asked again, just to be sure? If God tells you to do something, you better do it, right?

Jesus was in the Garden of Gethsemane, praying. He knew what was about to happen. He was going to be crucified on a cross. Even though Jesus knew what His future held, He was calling out to God, praying, and telling God He was sad. Jesus said to God, "If it is possible, let this cup pass." After calling out to God three times, Jesus said, "Your will be done." Jesus accepted what was about to happen to Him. One of Jesus' disciples, Judas, appeared in the garden and kissed Jesus on the cheek to betray Him. Jesus was arrested, and He knew exactly what was coming next. Even though Jesus knew what the future held, He was obedient and willingly followed God's plan.

Dear God,
Help me to always pray to You for guidance when I am scared or unsure of the future. Show me the plans You have for me so I may follow them. Amen.

CROSS CONNECTION

What are some of the emotions you think Jesus experienced during His time in the garden?

READ MATTHEW 27:32–44

Making a Mockery

Let's pretend you have a new friend who is visiting from another country. He might have an accent that makes his English difficult to understand. If you were to make fun of the way he spoke, that would be an example of making a mockery of someone.

Many people mocked Jesus after His arrest. He was judged and found guilty of nothing, but the people cried out for Him to be crucified. The crowd even chose to let a famous prisoner named Barabbas go free while demanding Jesus be crucified. Jesus was beaten, made fun of, and told to carry His cross to be crucified. He was so weak that another man was called in to carry the cross up the hill. A sign was placed above Jesus' head declaring Him "the King of the Jews." This sign wasn't meant as a compliment; it was meant to mock Him. The people wondered what real king would choose to stay on a cross and die if He had the power to escape.

Dear God,
Help me to remember how people treated Jesus on the cross. I want to treat others with love and kindness like You taught me to do. Amen.

CROSS CONNECTION

How do you think Jesus felt when He was on the cross and could hear people mocking Him?

*Above his head they put
up the charge against him
in writing:* THIS IS JESUS,
THE KING OF THE JEWS.
—MATTHEW 27:37

But JESUS cried out again with a loud voice and gave up his spirit. Suddenly, the curtain of the sanctuary was torn in two from top to bottom, the earth quaked, and the rocks were split. —MATTHEW 27:50–51

It Is Finished

First He was betrayed; then He was beaten and mocked; and finally Jesus was placed on a cross to die. Jesus knew what was coming, but the physical pain He experienced was horrible. At any moment, Jesus could have decided He'd had enough, and He could have gotten down from the cross and walked away. But Jesus stayed on the cross because He knew His purpose. He chose to bear the pain so that you could have the opportunity to choose a forever relationship with Him.

At the exact moment Jesus died, the curtain in the temple tore from the top to the bottom. The curtain wasn't needed anymore to separate a holy place from the rest of the temple. Jesus gave up His body on earth to pay for the sins of all people who would believe in Him. Jesus' dead body was removed from the cross and placed in a tomb. But the story doesn't end there. Tomorrow's reading, Matthew 28, delivers the best news ever.

Dear God,
Jesus didn't have to die for me, but He chose to. I don't ever want to forget the sacrifice He made. Help me to share the good news of Jesus' death and resurrection with others. Amen.

CROSS CONNECTION

Why do you think it is important to know that when Jesus died, the curtain in the temple tore from the top to the bottom?

READ MATTHEW 28:1–8

He Is Risen!

Mary Magdalene and another woman named Mary went to Jesus' tomb to prepare His body for burial. When they arrived, there was a violent earthquake. An angel of the Lord appeared and rolled away the stone covering the tomb where Jesus' body had been placed and guarded for three days. The angel then delivered the best news ever: "Jesus is alive. You won't find Him here. Go and tell everyone the good news. He is risen!" What an amazing moment!

Think about the nicest thing anyone has ever done for you. No matter what you thought of, it doesn't compare to what Jesus did for you. He endured physical pain, He was called names and made fun of, and He was crucified on a cross although He wasn't guilty of any crimes. Jesus chose to go through all of that because He loves you. He took your place when you belonged on the cross. You have the choice now. Will you follow the way to the Savior?

Dear God,
I am so grateful that Jesus is alive! Thank You for sending Him to save me from my sins. Help me to share the good news with others who need to hear more about You. Amen.

CROSS CONNECTION

Describe what you think it must have been like on the first Easter when people realized Jesus was alive.

He is not here. For he has risen, just as he said. Come and see the place where he lay. Then go quickly and tell his disciples, "He has risen from the dead and indeed he is going ahead of you to Galilee; you will see him there."
—Matthew 28:6–7

Memory Maker

As you go through the Lenten season, use these Memory Maker pages to write down the memories you share as a family. Be sure to include the date with each answer so you can return to this book each year as you celebrate Jesus and His love for your family.

How do you know Jesus loves you?

_____

_____

_____

_____

_____

_____

_____

_____

_____

_____

_____

_____

What did the members of your family choose to give up or add during this year's Lenten season?

_____

_____

_____

_____

_____

_____

_____

_____

_____

_____

_____

_____

_____

_____

_____

What did you wear on Easter Sunday? (Tape a picture to this page if you'd like.)

_____

_____

_____

_____

_____

_____

_____

_____

_____

_____

_____

_____

_____

_____

_____

What have you learned about your family while sharing this Lenten devotional?

_____

_____

_____

_____

_____

_____

_____

_____

_____

_____

_____

_____

_____

_____

_____

What activity did your family do together to remember Jesus during this Easter season?

_____

_____

_____

_____

_____

_____

_____

_____

_____

_____

_____

_____

_____

_____

_____

_____

What is your favorite Easter tradition?

_____

_____

_____

_____

_____

_____

_____

_____

_____

_____

_____

_____

_____

_____

_____

What food did you share for your Easter meal?

What chapter in this book was your favorite this year? Why?

Gather your family for some simple activities that can spark your creativity as well as create discussions around the Easter story.

Make a Salt Dough Tomb

Supplies: 1 cup salt, 2 cups flour, ¾ cup water

Instructions: Preheat the oven to 250 degrees. In a large bowl, mix salt and flour together. Gradually stir in water, mixing until it forms the consistency of dough. Use your hands to knead the mixture until it is no longer sticky. Allow your kids to create a tomb from the dough. Leave an opening for the tomb. Create a stone for the opening of the tomb. Place the tomb and stone on a baking sheet and set in the oven. Bake until hard, approximately 2.5 hours, depending on the thickness of the art. As a family, paint the tomb while you talk about the excitement the people must have felt when they discovered the tomb was empty.

Jesus' Last Days Murals

Supplies: sidewalk chalk

Instructions: Head to the driveway or a sidewalk to illustrate pictures of what Jesus' last days might have looked like. Direct your kids to draw the following:

• Jesus praying in the garden

• Jesus riding into Jerusalem on a donkey

• Jesus sharing the Last Supper with the disciples

• Jesus on the cross

• The empty tomb

Remind your kids that Jesus came to earth so that He could rescue people from their sins and allow them to live with God in heaven one day.

Easter Nature Walk

Supplies: copy paper, crayons

Instructions: Take your family on a nature walk to discover some items from the Easter story and create art rubbings. As you walk, look for the items in the list below.

- Coin: Remind your kids that Judas betrayed Jesus for 30 pieces of silver.
- Leaves: Discuss how people waved palm branches as Jesus entered Jerusalem.
- Bark of a tree: Tell your kids that the cross was made of wood.
- Footprint: For this one, you might need to do your rubbing on the bottom of a shoe. Share with your kids that Simon of Cyrene carried Jesus' cross when it became too heavy for Him.
- Flower: Remind your kids that Jesus died on the cross and was resurrected so that people could have new life in Him.

Once you bring your collected items home, use them to create art rubbings. Lay a piece of copy paper over each item, and rub the crayon over it to reveal the shape and features of the item.

Spice Painting

Supplies: tempera paint, kitchen spices or essential oils, poster paper, paintbrushes

Instructions: Pour different colors of tempera paint into individual paper cups or bowls. Add spices or essential oils to each color. The amount you add depends on how fragrant you want your paint to be. Allow kids to use the poster paper, paintbrushes, and spice-scented paints to create pictures that make them think about Easter. Remind the kids that the women who discovered the empty tomb thought they were going to put spices on Jesus' body as part of His burial process, but they had a wonderful surprise.

We hope this book will become part of your family tradition of remembering Jesus during the Easter season. Every year Lent begins and ends on a different date, so check the dates below to know when to begin.

2020	February 26
2021	February 17
2022	March 2
2023	February 22
2024	February 14
2025	March 5
2026	February 18
2027	February 10
2028	March 1
2029	February 14
2030	March 6